FIND A JOB ANYTIME, ANYWHERE

The Senior Professional's Guide to Job Search

RITA KAMEL

Find a Job Anytime, Anywhere The Senior Professional's Guide to Job Search Copyright © 2023 by Rita Kamel.

Website: https://www.dossierpro.co
Email: rita@dossierpro.co

To my job seeking community, my senior professionals, and clients from all around the world who are committed to their goals and hired me.

To my family, mentors, and friends who supported me in all my endeavors through thick and thin and keep encouraging me.

To my husband Georges and my daughter Neoma who always find the stamina and the words to keep me going and give me every reason to.

Thank you

TABLE OF CONTENTS

Section Four - Bouncing Back Faster and Stronger: Harnessing Motivation for Success

Bonus

WELCOME

If you want to be fully prepared for your next step, you've come to the right place!

Hello and welcome. My name is Rita Kamel and my mission is to empower senior professionals to lead their international career moves. I'm fluent in English, French, and Arabic. I'm a Master Certified Career and Employment Strategist with more than 15 years of experience in recruitment.

If you're looking to move forward or plan your transition, I'm here to help you achieve your goals. Ready for a session? Let's work together!

Who is this book for?

- This book is for you if you are a busy professional and you need information accessible anytime from anywhere.
- This book is for you if you are looking for straight-to-the-point information.
- This book is not for you if you want information about career exploration or employment interviews.
- This book is not for you if you want information about resume/CV, cover letter, or LinkedIn profile writing.

WHAT IS THE JOB SEARCH DASHBOARD?

As you go through the book, I invite you to fill the job search dashboard as a one document similar to a vision board, where you'd have all your answers in one visual right before your eyes.

The aim is to give you structure with a document that will act as a central repository. This quick access document will also provide you with personalized insights and may help you see links where you have not. It also captures the actions you've taken and the progress you've made.

I believe it's a valuable self-reflection tool where you can review your journey, and identify areas of growth just like you would on a business plan

Find a Job Anytime, Anywhere

THE JOB SEARCH DASHBOARD

YOUR GOAL
List the job titles you are searching for:

IDEAL WORK ENVIRONMENT
What does your ideal work environment look like?

YOUR VALUE PROPOSITION
List the problems you solve, who benefits from your work, and you are the person for the job. Include your added value and culture add. WHY you do what you do?

YOUR LIMITS
What are your limits?

YOUR COMPETENCIES
List the hard skills required by the job you want:

DEMOGRAPHICS
List the location of the job and work authorization barriers:

YOUR TARGETED COMPANIES
List the companies that fit your preferred demographics:

ADDITIONAL NOTES
Write any additional notes you may have:

SUMMARY OF QUALIFICATIONS
Highlight your strengths and talents but only those you enjoy and that are directly related to the job you are interested in:

www.dossierpro.co

9

SECTION ONE
IT STARTS WITH YOU:
EMPOWERING THE JOURNEY
OF SELF-AUDIT AND DISCOVERY

WHAT DOES YOUR SITUATION LOOK LIKE?

Let's take a moment to reflect on your current situation. I have a few questions to help you identify areas for improvement and create a plan to achieve your goals. But first, let me tell you the story of Laura.

Laura is a senior professional with 15 years of experience in her industry looking for her next career move. She felt stuck in her job search. She searched for a new job for several months, but nothing worked out. She felt frustrated and unsure of what steps to take next.

While working together, I asked her to reflect on her current situation and identify areas for improvement. Laura realized that she was feeling overwhelmed by the job search process and that she needed to focus on specific areas to make progress. She decided to spend more time networking and researching companies that aligned with her career goals.

As Laura reflected on the steps she had already taken, she noticed that she had been applying for jobs online without success. She decided to switch her approach and reach out to connections in her network for job opportunities. This worked well for her, and she received several job interviews as a result.

When she considered her biggest obstacle, she realized that it was her lack of confidence in her abilities. So, she decided to build her self-confidence by practicing positive self-talk and seeking feedback.

Finally, Laura envisioned her success by imagining herself in her dream job. She visualized the steps she would take to achieve her career goal, including continuing to network and build her skills.

With a clear plan in mind, she was able to move forward with renewed energy and purpose. Laura continued to reflect on her progress, adjust her plan as needed, and ultimately landed her dream job.

Now, it's your turn! Find a comfortable space to reflect, and be honest with yourself as you answer the following questions:

How do you feel about your current job search? Are you making progress, or feeling stuck?
Your answer:

What specific areas would you like to focus on over the next few weeks to move closer to your career goals?
Your answer:

What steps have you already taken to get closer to your goal?
Your answer:

What has worked well, and what could be improved?
Your answer:

What is your biggest obstacle to achieving your career goals, and how can you overcome it?
Your answer:

Finally, let's envision your success: Imagine that you have already achieved your career goal.

How did you get there? What specific actions did you take to make it a reality?
Your answer:

Use this vision to help guide your plan moving forward.

WHAT DOES YOUR IDEAL ENVIRONMENT LOOK LIKE?

Aligning your personal goals and values with those of the organization is crucial for a fulfilling career. Not every workplace will be the right fit for you, and it's important to recognize this to avoid wasting your time and energy pursuing opportunities that don't align with your aspirations.

To ensure that you're connecting with the right employer, it's essential to be focused and clear on what you want. This will help you make informed decisions throughout the recruitment process.

Now, let me tell you about Sarah. Sarah has been working in a traditional corporate environment for decades but was feeling unfulfilled. She realized that she wanted to work for a company that encouraged creativity and innovation but wasn't sure where to start her search.

So, I sat with her and asked her a few questions. She said she wanted to work for a startup with an entrepreneurial philosophy that valued open communication and employee autonomy. She also realized that she wanted to work with people who were passionate and driven, as she believed this would inspire her to be her best self.

Through her research, Sarah found a startup that aligned with her values and was in need of her expertise. She took the opportunity and was thrilled to find that she was finally working in an environment that aligned with her personal goals and values.

Now, let's take action to identify YOUR ideal workplace. Get specific and detailed in your answers, and be sure to elaborate on your reasoning.

Here are some questions to help guide you:

What are your ideal companies, and where are they located? Make a list.
Your answer:

What position would you like to hold, and why?
Your answer:

Do you prefer to work in a startup, mid-sized, or large corporation, and why?
Your answer:

Which organizational philosophy and style are you seeking? Traditional or entrepreneurial, and why?
Your answer:

What workplace values are essential for you, and why?
Your answer:

What type of personalities do you prefer to work with, and why?
Your answer:

How are communications and conflict handled in your ideal workplace, and why is this important to you?
Your answer:

What is the frequency of interaction between leaders and employees, and why is this important to you?
Your answer:

By answering these questions, you'll gain clarity on what you're looking for and be better equipped to identify and pursue opportunities that align with your career goals and values.

WHAT ARE YOUR LIMITS?

I think that not all jobs are a one-size-fits-all solution. We're all unique individuals with different backgrounds, financial situations, and goals. So, what works for one person might not work for another.

For example, the current trend in some places is to offer a contract before a permanent position, which might not be the best solution for everyone. This could mean fewer benefits which might be a dealbreaker.

Some people prioritize work-life balance over high pay, while others prioritize earning potential over their personal life. For some, like me working remotely is a must-have, while for others, being in the office is essential for collaboration and networking.

So, let's define what you're comfortable with in your job search. By doing so, you can differentiate between a "Hell, yes!" and a "Hell, no!" opportunity.

Take a few minutes to answer some questions and help narrow down your job search:

Do you value job security over career fulfillment? Or would you rather seek out temporary contracts that offer valuable experience but less stability?
Your answer:

What types of work are you willing to consider, even if they're not your ideal job? And why do you think so?
Your answer:

On the other hand, what types of work are you unwilling to consider, no matter what? Why is that?
Your answer:

How comfortable are you with taking a risk on a short-term contract if it means turning down a more stable job? What are your thoughts on that?
Your answer:

Answering these questions will give you a clearer idea of your job search priorities and help you make informed decisions about your career.

WHAT ARE YOUR VALUES?

Have you ever found yourself feeling stressed or unfulfilled in your career? It's natural to feel that way when our actions do not align with our values. That's why it's important to take some time to reflect on what really matters to you in your career.

Values are the answer to the questions:

What's important to you in your career? *Your answer:*

What is your purpose? *Your answer:*

What do you enjoy doing? *Your answer:*

When do you feel satisfied and fulfilled? *Your answer:*

You can think of your values as a compass that makes navigating a job search project a little easier. We tend to be happier, more fulfilled, and less overwhelmed in difficult situations when we know our values and live in line with them.

When we make decisions or act in ways that dishonour our values, we can feel stressed, anxious, and generally unhappy.

For example, if you value family but spend most of your time on business trips or working 60 hours a week, how do you think this imbalance between your values and your actions might feel?

By choosing and prioritizing your values, you know where to invest your time and effort in the future so that you can be the kind of person you want to be.

We will be doing three exercises to get clear on your values

Exercise 1: Your Top 5 Values

Before we start looking at your values, let's consider some common examples of values. Here is a list to give you a clear idea of what values are.

Acceptance
Achievement
Advancement
Affection
Altruism
Community
Competence
Competition
Creativity
Discovery
Equality
Excitement
Fairness
Fame
Family Happiness
Freedom
Friendship
Fun
Growth
Health
Helping Others
Honesty
Integrity
Money
Peace
Personal Development

Pleasure
Power
Privacy
Spirituality
Status
Success
Teaching
Wealth
Wisdom

Now take some time to brainstorm about your values. Select your top 5 values and write them down by order of importance.

It can be difficult to choose only 5, because you may feel that there are so many others that are equally important to you.

The following question may help you to prioritize them. Ask yourself: "Which value can I not be without?"

Enter the name of the value and write down what this value means to you.

For example, if you have entered "success" in the previous question, what does success mean to you?

Write value #1 and what it means to you:
Your answer:

Write value #2 and what it means to you:
Your answer:

Write value #3 and what it means to you:
Your answer:

Write value #4 and what it means to you:
Your answer:

Write value #5 and what it means to you:
Your answer:

Exercise 2: The Farewell Party

If you were given a farewell party...

How would you want to be remembered by those with whom you worked?
Your answer:

What would you want them to say about you?
Your answer:

Exercise 3: Your Last Day On Earth

In this exercise, you are going to explore your core values. For example, someone with a core value of courage is likely to actively seek new challenges despite the possibility of failure or rejection. In essence, your values are what make you, you. Living your values means knowing what you stand for and acting in ways that align with them. When your actions match your values, you are happier and generally more content. This exercise will help you connect with your core values by reflecting on your imagined last day on Earth.

Think about your last day on Earth. Get comfortable, take a few slow, deep breaths, and allow your eyes to close gently. Now, imagine that you have only one day left on the planet. Perhaps you are boarding a spaceship destined to explore the galaxy, or maybe an asteroid is on a collision course and headed for impact; no matter the backstory, tomorrow will be your last day here on Earth.

After tomorrow, you will be gone forever. As you think about your last hours on the planet, look deep inside yourself and try to create as vivid an image as possible.

Engage your senses.

What do you feel? What thoughts pop up in your mind?
Your answer:

Your values may have changed while going through this process. However, now you have your solid 5 values.

Remember, your values may change over time, and that's okay. But having clarity on what matters to you can help guide your job search and decision-making process. So, take some time to complete these exercises and get clear on your values.

YOUR SOLID 5 VALUES

Your answer:

WHAT ARE YOUR STRENGTHS?

Strengths are things at which we are naturally good. For instance, we might be naturally creative, particularly generous with our time, or persevere when things get tough. Using our strengths energizes us and helps us feel and perform at our best. I invite you to get through the three exercises to identify your unique gifts.

Exercise 1: The Strengths Interview.

During this interview, you'll answer questions about things that are related to the core characteristics of strengths, namely energy, performance, and authenticity.

Please note that these questions don't have a right or wrong answer. It is, however, important that you answer the questions honestly.

If you find it difficult to answer a question, you can skip it.

What do you like to do?
Your answer:

At what times do you feel fully engaged?
Your answer:

When do you lose track of time?
Your answer:

When do you feel like the "real you"?
Your answer:

What have you learned quickly, catching on with minimal effort?
Your answer:

What are you looking forward to in the future?
Your answer:

What brings positive energy into your life?
Your answer:

What are your interests?
Your answer:

What other careers have you considered but did not pursue?
Your answer:

List anything that comes to mind. Think about everything you spend time researching or reading or talking about.

Exercise 2: Exploring Flow Experiences

Sometimes when we are engaged in something, we may find that we have completely lost track of time. We are engrossed in what we are doing and intensely enjoy it. In positive psychology, this concept is called "flow".

A flow state occurs when you are intensely focused on the present moment. Your focus becomes so deep that you are effortlessly involved in what you are doing. Nothing else seems to matter.

The activity that you are involved in - this may be a sport, another hobby, or something you do at work - is intrinsically rewarding. This means that you engage in it because you love the activity, not because you want to achieve some outcome or get positive feedback from others.

Flow is one of life's highly enjoyable states of being, wrapping us entirely in the present, and helping us be more creative, productive, and happy. In this exercise, we are going to further explore your own experiences of a flow state.

Think of a time when you were in a flow state: you were completely absorbed and focused on what you were doing, you felt positive and secure about your abilities, and were not worried about failing.

Take some time to recall this event.

When did you have this experience?
Your answer:

What was going on?
Your answer:

Where were you?
Your answer:

How or what did you feel?
Your answer:

How did you feel after the experience was over?
Your answer:

Are there more examples of activities that you recognize as flow states in your life? What are they?
Your answer:

Do the examples that you mention share a specific characteristic? For instance, creativity may be involved in all or most of the examples. Maybe the activities are always carried out alone or on the contrary, always with others.
Your answer:

Would it be possible to do the flow activities that you mentioned more often? If so, what could be the first step to doing these activities more often?
Your answer:

Exercise 3: Signs You've Found Your Unique Talent

Here are some signs that you've found your unique talent:

- It feels fun and easy.
- You can do it for hours and are more energized, not less.
- Time collapses around you - you lose track of the hours when you are engaged in your natural talent.
- You create superior results with less effort.
- You add value effortlessly to those around you.
- It is easy to be successful.
- You are happy and fulfilled.
- You feel fully alive and self-expressed.

If you feel that something is missing or that you haven't tapped into your full potential, then you have more discovery work to do!

Here are some questions you can reflect on:

Are you an extrovert or an introvert?
Your answer:

Are you a tactical thinker or a strategic thinker?
Your answer:

Do you prefer to do one thing at a time or to multitask?
Your answer:

Are you hands-on or hands-off?
Your answer:

Are you quick to anger or slow to anger?
Your answer:

Here are questions you can ask your family, friend, and coworkers:

What do you think is my greatest strength?
Your answer:

What is my biggest weakness? Ask this because typically, the flip side of your greatest strength there is your greatest weakness. If you can readily imagine five to ten years into the future, you may not be so proficient at dealing with the task at hand today and find that you procrastinate.
Your answer:

What do you see as my special talent, ability, or gift?
Your answer:

What do I do naturally and effortlessly that is special?
Your answer:

This is a really fun one: **If I were on the cover of a magazine, what magazine would it be, and what would the article be about?**
Your answer:

When am I most fully expressing this talent, gift, or ability?
Your answer:

Wooh! Too many questions, huh? So, tell me now, what did you discover?
Your answer:

HOW TO PUT THINGS TOGETHER?

You've done a lot of good work answering many questions. I know, I know, it's one thing to ask questions, and it's another to reflect on them. But hey, you're gaining momentum and you are moving forward through a series of small actions one step at a time!

Let's mix three ingredients together and make some magic. We'll need your answers to the strengths, values, and ideal work environment exercises.

Using your strengths, make a sentence that speaks to what you do.

Example: I deliver and implement complex large-scale projects by leading teams using coaching and empathy. I love to solve problems by analyzing data and setting the best strategy.

Now it's your turn: **I....** *Your answer:*

Then let's expand further by adding values and ideal work environment. **I value...** *Your answer:*

I do this well where... *Your answer:*

See? Now you have a sentence that you can use when you engage in job search-related conversations!

SECTION TWO
UNVEILING NEW OPPORTUNITIES:
EMBRACING THE MODERN APPROACH

HOW CAN LINKEDIN SUPPORT YOUR JOB SEARCH?

LinkedIn is a tool that is massively used for a number of purposes. From job search to networking and selling; LinkedIn is used by millions of people worldwide.

It can assist you in YOUR job search in many different ways; but in order to see results, you need to first make sure that you have a complete profile with a banner, a professional photograph, a compelling headline, an attractive and detailed About and Experience section as well as thoroughly developed other sections. That being said it's time to access the tool and take some additional steps.

I would like you to go on LinkedIn to both find and follow the companies you are interested to work in. Here, you can be very selective.

Find and make a list of at least 5 to 10 people who work in each of the companies you are interested to work in.
Your answer:

Write a short outreach message of 300 characters maximum to send out when you send a connection request to these people. (NB: I would recommend doing this on a laptop/desktop because on mobile this step is skipped when you click "Connect") The outreach message should state the reason why you are connecting.
Your answer:

Here are some examples:

- Hi [Name], I'm landing in [City] in [Month] and I would love to connect with you as a peer in my industry to have your insights on the challenges to expect.

- Hi [Name], I'm a [Your job title] landing in [City] in [Month]. I'm looking to expand my network & connect with you to learn more about the current industry challenges. Would you be open to sharing some insights? Thank you for your time!

-Hi [Name] I'm an aspiring [title] looking to get into [company they work at]. I have applied online and reached out to recruiter [Name], but I'd love to get your advice as you have successfully made it. I appreciate any tips & advice you may have. Would you be open to sharing your insights?

- Hi [recruiter's name], I'm a [job title] interested in learning more about the [open position] role. I applied online & found your profile which said you're the recruiter. I'd like to express my interest directly & would be happy to set up a call to discuss further. I'd really appreciate it!

Always edit and adjust to fit your specific case and personalize your message as much as possible. Don't expect everyone to reply. This part is a numbers game; the more people you connect with, the more replies you will receive. After connecting with all the people and companies of interest you will start gaining visibility, and visitors will check your profile and what you are writing about... hmm... so what are you writing about?

Take a moment to brainstorm about a few topics you could write content about to position yourself as someone who is an expert in their field. Take the habit to post regularly and consistently to gain traction. Even if it's just once a week, stick to it, it will create momentum.

Also don't forget to comment on other's people posts with thoughtful, constructive feedback and insights which will spark their curiosity and bring more visitors to your profile.

WHAT IS AN INFORMATIONAL INTERVIEW AND HOW TO USE IT?

What is an informational interview?

An informational interview is one of the most valuable sources of occupational information. While the conversation may cover some of the same ground information on a company website, it not only presents opportunities for a flexible inside view of a job field unmatched by other sources, but it also presents the opportunity to network for job search and remain on top of mind for a desired internal referral.

This type of interview is conducted to collect information about a job, career field, industry, or company. It is NOT a job interview. Instead, it's an opportunity to speak with a person working in a field you'd like to know more about. Through an informational interview, you can find out about a specific job type, a person's career path, or details on an industry or company.

Through the conversation, you can (hopefully) discover what a person's job is like, what they do, what responsibilities they have, and what it's like to work in their job at their company.

It is useful whether you are a career changer or a job seeker because you are introducing yourself as well to people in companies of interest.

How to Find People to Speak With?

Your network can help. Depending on how secret your job search is, you can reach out to friends, family, and acquaintances to see if they know anyone in the industry, you're interested in exploring and can make a connection.

If there is a specific company you'd like to work in, consider cold-contacting someone through LinkedIn to request an informational interview. You can also follow up with people you met during networking events or job fairs.

Perfect The Art of the Ask

Any cold email has two things: a clear message (why you're reaching out), and an easy-to-understand ask (the action you want the recipient to take). Here is a simple formula that checks both boxes and that will work most of the time:

Start by asking for help: This sounds obvious, but it's a proven fact that people love to feel like they are helping others. So, if you start by saying, "I'd love your help," or "I hope you'll be able to help me out..." your chances of getting a positive response go up significantly.

Be clear: Ask for something very specific, and make it as easy as possible for the person to say yes. Saying, "I'd love to know more about what you do and how you got your start" is okay, but doesn't tell how much of their time you're after or what you're suggesting. Instead, try something like, "I'd love to take you to a quick coffee so I can hear your perspective on this industry and what it's like to work at your company. I'll be in your area next week and would be happy to meet you wherever is convenient for you." (Of course, adjust your message if you want to meet virtually.

Have a hook: A great way to increase your chance of landing the interview is to demonstrate why you want to meet with this person. Do you admire their career path? Maybe you have a shared connection and think they would be a great voice of wisdom. Don't be afraid to share why you are reaching out specifically to this person. The more personalized your ask feels the greater chance of success you'll have.

Be very considerate: Remember that in asking for an informational interview, you're asking someone to put their work on hold to help you. Show your contact you understand this by saying, "I can only imagine how busy you must get, so even 15-20 minutes would be so appreciated."

Make sure you don't seem like you're looking for a job (even if you are): If you sound like you're just looking for a job, there's a good chance this person will push you to HR or the company's career page. Be sure to make it clear that you want to talk to them, to learn about their career history and perspective on the job or industry. After you meet and make a great impression is when you can mention the job hunt.

Follow-up, and be pleasantly persistent: If you don't hear back right away, don't worry. People are busy, and sometimes these things slip to the bottom of a person's to-do list. The key is not to give up. If you haven't heard back in a week, reply to your first email and politely ask if your contact has had a chance to read your previous email. Also, use this opportunity to reiterate how much it would mean to you to have 15 minutes to learn from them. It's your responsibility to continue to follow up (as nicely as possible) every couple of weeks until you've heard an answer one way or the other. Some would say that after one or two tries, you may run the risk of upsetting the person, but sometimes, persistence pays off. At the end of the day, it's really up to you and your comfort level.

It's also worth noting that not every informational interview needs to be a live call, video call, or even coffee meeting. The ask and questions can be simply sent via email or private message. Remember that most people are happy to help once you reach out to them.

HOW TO CONDUCT AN INFORMATIONAL INTERVIEW?

You should regard each informational interview as a business appointment and professionally conduct yourself.

If you have made clear, in advance, the explicit purpose of your interview you will, in all probability, find your contact an interested and helpful person.

Remember the appointment time and appear promptly for your interview You should neither be too casually dressed nor overdressed. Be sure you know the name of the person you are meeting, the correct pronunciation of their name, and the title of their position. Do some research on the person and their company.

Come with questions, and be prepared to steer the conversation. Be sure to be considerate of the person's time. Aim to keep the conversation brief (about 15 to 30 minutes) unless you've agreed on a different time frame beforehand. And, remember: your contact might ask you questions as well Be ready with an elevator pitch.

Informational Interview Questions to Ask

Come prepared with a number of occupational and functional questions Because there are so many questions you can ask in the informational interview, individuals sometimes take notes during the meeting. A limited amount of note-taking is justified provided that your contact is agreeable and that it doesn't interrupt communication between the two of you.

During the interview, try to ask questions that go beyond what you could find out through a quick online search. You can ask the person about their journey to this position, for a description of their day-to-day responsibilities, and for tips they would offer you as someone interested in working in the field.

After the interview, sketch out a brief outline of the topics covered and the information you discovered. This will require only a few minutes and will ensure that you remember the important points discussed. Later, working from your outline, you can construct a more detailed report of the interview.

Occupational Questions to Ask

- What are the duties performed during a typical day, week, month, or year? Do they have a set routine? How much variety is there on a day-to-day basis? As the person describes the duties, ask what skills are needed.
- What educational program is recommended as preparation? Inquire about the distinction between desirable courses and those which are indispensable.
- What degree or certificate or certification do employers look for?
- What kind of work experience would employers look for in a job applicant, and how does a person obtain this experience?
- What are the opportunities for advancement, and to what position? Is an advanced degree needed?
- Which skills are most important to acquire?
- What are the main, or most important, personal characteristics for success in the field?
- What other kinds of workers frequently interact with this position?
- What are the employment prospects in your geographic area? Where are the best employment prospects? What are the employment prospects at the advisor's company?
- Is mobility a necessary factor for success?
- What are the demands and frustrations that typically accompany this type of work?

- Is there a typical chain of command in this field?
- How can you determine that you have the ability or potential to be successful in this specific occupation?
- Is this a rapidly growing field? Is it possible to predict future needs for workers in this field?
- What types of technology are used and how are they used?

Functional Questions to Ask

- What are the satisfying aspects of the advisor's work?
- What are the greatest pressures, strains, or anxieties in the work?
- What are the major job responsibilities?
- What are the toughest problems and decisions with which you must cope?
- What is most dissatisfying about the work?
- How would you describe the atmosphere/culture of the workplace?

Follow-up with a Thank You Note

Write a Thank You note to the people you have interviewed. Report back to them if you have followed up on any suggestions. You can also connect with them on LinkedIn if you have not already. Here is an example:

Dear [Name of person you interviewed with],

Thank you for meeting with me today to talk about your work as [Name of Company]'s [Position]. I now have a much better understanding of the field, particularly ......
It was helpful to hear that ....
I have decided to.......
I have also contacted your colleague.... to set up a meeting to speak with them.
I very much appreciate having had the opportunity to talk with you. Thank you again for your time and advice.

Sincerely, [Your name]

HOW TO CREATE MORE OPTIONS?

You've probably heard the advice to "cast a wide net" when looking for your next job. What does it mean and how do you do it?

As with any project, it all starts with an evaluation to see what you really enjoy. Casting a wide net is not a coincidence, it is a search focused on new areas.

Option 1: Area Expansion

One of the easiest ways to broaden your search is to look beyond your current geographic boundaries. Another city or even another country.

Let me share with you John's experience: After working as a Software Developer in a small town for several years, John had become frustrated with the limited job opportunities available in his area. He decided to cast a wide net and explore job opportunities in different cities. He applied for jobs in several different locations and was offered a position at a large software company in Toronto.

Moving to a new city was challenging, but John was excited about the opportunity to work in a larger company and collaborate with other developers who shared his passion for programming. He quickly settled into his new job and found that the change of scenery had reignited his passion for software development.

Option 2: Professional Expansion

Find out how your job has changed and how other companies are naming your role. Networking can shed light on things. Some jobs do no longer exist. Other professions have grown to include many different job responsibilities. Most jobs require the latest technical skills and various qualifications. You will need to target your career documents to make sure that your message is focused.

This is what happened with Lucy. Lucy had been working as a Graphic Designer for a marketing agency for several years, but she was feeling unfulfilled in her current role. She decided to explore different job opportunities and found that many companies were looking for candidates with a broader skill set, including experience in web design and user experience.

Lucy decided to cast a wide net and expand her professional skills by enrolling in a course on web design and user experience. She also began networking with professionals in these fields and attending industry events to learn more about the latest trends and technologies. With her expanded skill set and industry knowledge, she was able to land a job at a tech startup as a Product Designer, where she was able to use her skills in a more fulfilling way.

Option 3: Industry Expansion

The things you enjoy and the skills you've developed may be needed in other industries. Conduct your research and engage in networking activities. Ask questions such as: "These are things I really enjoy. What do you call them at your company?" or "One of the things I'm really good at is helping people solve actuarial problems. What type of people solve these problems at your company?" Then, put some of these skills into the keyword search section of some of the frequently used job boards to see what kind of companies pop up. You can also further network to request informational interviews to learn more about the requirements of this job at this industry.

Mark did exactly that. After working as an Accountant for several years, Mark was feeling unfulfilled in his current job and was considering a career change. He decided to cast a wide net and explore different industries where his skills might be applicable. He began researching different industries and found that the healthcare industry was in need of financial analysts with his skill set.

Mark began networking with professionals in the healthcare industry and attending industry events to learn more about the job requirements and opportunities. He discovered that his experience was highly transferable and he was able to land a job in a large hospital.

Having more options can give you more control over your job search project and make you feel energized.

What are your expansion options?

- **Area Expansion.** *Your answer:*
- **Professional Expansion.** *Your answer:*
- **Industry Expansion.** *Your answer:*

HOW TO MANAGE YOUR ONLINE REPUTATION?

As you probably know, employers often do their research online before making a hiring decision. This means that it's important to be mindful of what potential employers might see when they look you up online.

So, what can you do to manage your online reputation during your job search? Here are some tips:

Google yourself: Do a quick search of your name and see what comes up. Are there any results that you wouldn't want a potential employer to see? If so, you may want to consider taking steps to remove or hide those results.

If the result is on a website that you have control over, such as a personal blog or social media profile, you can simply remove the content. If the result is on a website that you don't have control over, you can try reaching out to the website owner and asking them to remove the content. If that isn't an option, you can try burying the result by creating new, positive content about yourself that ranks higher in search results.

Clean up your social media profiles: Make sure that your social media profiles, especially LinkedIn, are professional and up to date. Remove any inappropriate or unprofessional photos, posts, and comments. Make sure that your profiles accurately reflect your current job experience and skills.

Build a positive online presence: Consider creating a personal website or blog where you can showcase your work and expertise. This can help to establish you as an industry thought leader and can be a great way for potential employers to learn more about you.

Be mindful of what you post online: Always think before you post. Ask yourself if the content you are sharing is something that you would be comfortable with a potential employer seeing. Remember that once something is online, it can be very difficult to remove it.

Keep an eye on your online reputation: Use tools like Google Alerts to monitor what is being said about you online. This can help you to stay on top of any potential issues and address them quickly.

By following these tips, you can help to ensure that your online reputation is a positive one and that it doesn't hold you back during your job search.

SECTION THREE
MASTERING THE INSIDE INSIGHT:
NAVIGATING ONLINE AND OFFLINE JOB SEARCH

WHY IS NETWORKING IMPORTANT?

Networking enables you to take advantage of personal and business connections, rather than relying solely on your resume. These connections are not only beneficial for you but also for employers, who hire many new employees through networking.

Companies want to hire the best person for the job. There is pressure on those leading the hiring process to find someone who has the skills and experience necessary to succeed in the position and who the employer will like and trust. While interviewing based on resumes alone can help employers find strong candidates, relying on networks and the networks of their employees can reduce the risk of a bad hire. Trust me, I was a Recruiter for 15 years!

Using networking to get a job interview means you'll enter the hiring process with a relationship and level of trust with your employer, thanks to your network. Networking to find a job can also give you access to opportunities that you may not find in an online job search. Many positions, especially the very senior ones, are usually not listed on company websites but are instead shared only internally or through networking. This means that you need to regularly communicate with those in your network so they know your skills and your experience, trust you and know when you are in search of a job.

Networking for a job requires strategic thinking and developing skills that help you connect with others. By networking efficiently, you can guarantee that the effort you put into cultivating these relationships is worth your time and the time of your colleagues.

Here are a few tips to consider when networking for your next job:

Offer help: You can improve your relationships with your contacts and your chances of finding work by offering to help your contacts. Remember that networking is about turning outwards, and volunteering to help your connections can illustrate your motivation and dedication and may even allow you to display your skills. Listen to your connections and look for opportunities to help regardless of whether they are guaranteeing you a position in their company. They may remember your assistance and recommend you for a position in the future.

Fight your fear: If you are an introvert, you may need to challenge yourself to be more outgoing to network effectively. Encourage yourself to do a little more than you normally would by speaking to someone a little longer or interacting with a handful of people at your next work event. If you are anxious about interacting with others, try preparing questions and discussion topics before talking with them. You may also be hesitant to network for fear of rejection. Try to be proud of your efforts regardless of the outcome, and remember that you will have more opportunities to create connections that may lead to the job you want.

Be patient and make time: Cultivating strong relationships can take time, as can networking to find the right position. You will likely need to be patient as you meet with connections and make new ones. It can also be helpful to call a company you're interested in working for and ask for an informational meeting. Go with the intent of getting to know the company and potential hiring managers, instead of planning to ask for a job. Taking that time can help build new relationships and familiarize yourself with your potential employers.

Focus on the relationship, not your resume: Even though it is tempting to focus on selling yourself and sharing your resume with everyone who will take it, focusing on relationships may make a more powerful impression than your previous work experience. Present yourself as a likable person before showing your professional worth.

Use social networks and online resources: Networking through face-to-face interaction is invaluable, but if you want to maximize your reach, use social networks and other online resources to reinforce relationships and search for new connections. In some cases, meeting face-to-face with employees of your target company may not be possible, but the internet can close the distance. Online contacts are a simple way to make initial connections.

Follow-up: Following up is an essential step in guaranteeing that your networking interactions were worthwhile. Follow-up with new connections after making initial contact. This follow-up can involve thanking them for meeting with you, asking further questions or sending along an article relevant to your conversation. These continued interactions strengthen the relationship, remind the contact of your meeting and perhaps cause them to think of you for an open position. A friend may also recommend contacting one of their connections. After reaching out to that contact, email your friend and do so again after you've received a response. This shows gratitude and strengthens your relationship by continuing to involve them in your journey.

HOW TO SEARCH FOR A JOB ONLINE AND OFFLINE?

You may notice that not all job openings get posted publicly. Instead, employers may only offer particular job opportunities to their internal employees or use recruiters to find external candidates. Utilizing your professional connection and networking abilities can help you tap into this hidden job market.

What is the hidden job market?

The hidden job market refers to jobs that employers do not advertise or publish publicly. Not publicizing these openings can help these employers save on the costs and time associated with posting and evaluating job applications or interviewing. To fill these jobs, employers may hire internally or use employee referral programs to find external candidates. Beyond saving costs, this method can help ensure high-quality candidates because employees already understand the company's expectations. This knowledge can enable them to move into that role themselves or recommend appropriate candidates.

How to access the hidden job market?

Tapping into the hidden job market requires networking effectively to build your connections and learn about unseen opportunities.

You can use the following advice as guidance for building your network and gaining access to hidden jobs:

Explore your current company: If you are looking for a change but enjoy working at your current company, you can ask around about internal opportunities elsewhere. Part of the hidden job market comprises companies with job openings intended for internal candidates. Connect with colleagues in departments that interest you and ask if they have any current or upcoming openings. Continue developing these relationships and staying in touch even if they do not have anything immediately. Your connection and demonstrated interest could lead them to contact you when an opportunity arises. Because you already have a job at the company, try to conduct this process discreetly. Depending on your relationship with your supervisor, you may not want them to know that you are looking elsewhere. However, when an opening arises that you would like to apply to, have a conversation with them about your intentions. Be sure to focus on the positive aspects of the change, such as the new opportunities it provides, rather than discussing why you dislike your current job. They will appreciate the honesty, and it can help them prepare to fill your place when the timing is right.

Reaching out to existing contacts: Share your goal of finding a new job with your professional and personal connections. Help them by being specific about the types of jobs you are seeking or your preferred professional fields. If they do not know of existing opportunities at their companies, they can contact you if something comes up. Or they may be able to connect you to someone at another company with openings. To keep these connections strong, interact with them regularly by sending them friendly messages or sharing content you think they may appreciate. Consistent communication helps to keep you on top of their mind.

Join networking groups: You can find networking groups related to your geographic area or your specific profession. These groups often serve as a resource for making new connections via regular meetings or networking events. Because the other networking group members are also seeking work, they may be eager to discuss advice for finding and applying for job opportunities. And they may hear about hidden jobs outside their areas of interest that they can share.

Think of finding a new job as a collaborative effort: Try to share insights you learn with your new networking connections to aid their searches, too. People may be more receptive to giving information or advice when they know you would do the same for them. As with your other professional connections, continue to stay in touch even after finding employment. You never know if someone will get a job at a company that you may want to work for in the future.

Utilize professional organizations: You can also learn about potential opportunities via alumni associations. Fellow alumni sometimes provide access to job openings not posted publicly. You can also join professional associations focused on your profession or field of interest. Companies in the industry may reach out to associations before posting openings publicly. These professional organizations also offer events to build your network with industry peers or alumni who work for your desired companies. These relationships can provide advice for your search and potentially connect you to hidden opportunities.

Stay active on social media: Many of today's employers have social media profiles, so make sure to follow and connect with those who interest you most. You can also use them to identify key employees in the company. Try to build connections with these figures by engaging with their content regularly and respectfully, providing unique insights, when possible, to demonstrate your industry knowledge. If you can develop a rapport with these figures, you can reach out to them and express your interest and ask for an informational interview. Remember to keep your social media profiles up-to-date with information about your current or most recent job responsibilities, accomplishments and skills. Stay active by joining and participating in online groups related to your industry, along with posting original, relevant content on your profile. These tactics can help you stay engaged in your professional community and build your network. When your connections see your activity and expertise, it can help you make an impression that could lead to potential opportunities.

Connect with Recruiters: Some employers use internal or external recruiters to find candidates for non-posted jobs. You can sometimes research and discover their internal recruiters via social media. If you decide to reach out to them, avoid asking for a job immediately. Try to build a rapport first, and discuss the reasons behind your interest in the company. Then you can mention some of your relevant and beneficial skills. Match their level of engagement and give them sufficient time to respond. You do not want to overwhelm them by sending too many messages or pushing for a response. Otherwise, you can learn about recruiting firms within your industry and connect with them. Many recruiters use social media to find candidates, which is another reason for staying active and keeping your profile updated. They may look within online groups or perform keyword searches. Make it clear what type of job you want or your industry of interest to aid their search. Try to use keywords from a public job posting to fill out your profile and demonstrate that you have the relevant skills and qualifications.

Contact employers directly: Rather than waiting for a job to open up at your dream company, you can show initiative by reaching out directly. When possible, use existing connections to point you in the direction of the appropriate Hiring Manager or do research to find them. To contact them, you can send an email or letter of interest or make a cold call. If you notice they are active on social media, you can even send them a private message to start a conversation. When cold contacting a Hiring Manager, introduce yourself and showcase the skills, experiences and accomplishments that make you fit at their company. To do this effectively, research the company to learn how you align with its mission, values and culture. You can typically find this information on company websites, social media profiles or employee review websites. Because you are not reaching out for a specific job opening, you can research individuals who hold roles that interest you. Identify the skills that you share and mention them to demonstrate your value.

Pursue volunteering opportunities: You can find volunteering opportunities related to your profession or personal interests. If you discover opportunities at companies you want to work for, it can help you make internal connections and demonstrate your enthusiasm for their mission or values. Your volunteer work can also display the value and dedication you could bring as a full-time employee. Pursuing volunteering opportunities related to your passions can also serve as an effective networking method. You can meet various people with similar interests who work in your preferred field or for companies you respect. As you build these relationships, you can demonstrate your interest in a new job and learn if they have any openings. Having referrals from internal employees can help make you stand out amongst other potential candidates.

Attend industry events: Pay attention to events related to your industry or profession, which you may hear about from the groups you belong to or your professional connections. Conferences or trade shows serve as opportunities to meet industry peers and decision-makers. Try to research the companies and attendees and set goals for yourself to focus your networking. When you plan the connections you want to make, it can help you use your time at the conference more efficiently. It can also help you plan out your conversation or elevator pitch to leave a memorable impression. During your conversations, you can mention your interest in finding a new job or working for their company. If the other person seems receptive to your interest, you can share business cards or contact information. Try to make a note to follow up within a week to discuss the idea further or set up an informational meeting. Your attendance at these events can also make an impression on a potential employer. It demonstrates your interest in growing your industry knowledge and developing professionally.

Stay current on news: To stay up-to-date on the companies you want to work for, set up news alerts. While these alerts may not point you toward posted job openings, they can provide insights into company changes. An article about a company's plans to open a new office can demonstrate that they may soon be hiring new employees. With this awareness, you can start reaching out to existing connections at the company or making new ones. If you get an informational interview or job interview, you can use these insights to demonstrate your interest and knowledge.

Am I saying that you won't find a job unless you network? No.
Am I saying that all senior jobs are not posted online? Also, no.

Depending on the company's location and size, different rules and regulations may apply. Some companies MUST post ALL their open positions online, but many others, simply don't.

I strongly suggest developing a balanced strategy that includes all the elements necessary for a shorter job search and go with whatever suits your case by applying online AND networking especially when looking for a job in a different country. Using these strategies, some of my clients and I had jobs specifically created for us.

Please always be aware of scams! Canada alone lost $7 Million to job scams in 2022.

Zombie Companies

As a job seeker, be cautious of companies that may not be financially stable in the long term. Zombie companies, which are firms that are unable to cover their debt obligations with their current profits, may offer job opportunities in the short term but could lead to layoffs or bankruptcies in the future.

Before accepting a job offer, research the company's financial statements and credit ratings. Check for any news articles or reports on the company's financial stability. Look for indicators such as declining revenue or mounting debt, which may suggest that the company is struggling financially.

Check the company's reputation online by reading reviews on websites like Glassdoor or Indeed. Look for any red flags such as a high employee turnover rate or negative reviews from former employees.

Consider working for companies in industries that are less vulnerable to economic downturns. For example, healthcare, technology, and renewable energy are all growing industries in Canada that are less likely to be impacted by economic crises.

Look for job opportunities that have the potential for long-term growth and stability. Ask about the company's plans for growth and expansion and whether they have a solid plan in place to achieve those goals.

Building your skills and expertise can make you more marketable to employers. Consider taking courses or certifications in in-demand fields, or gaining experience through internships or volunteering.

During the job interview process, trust your gut instinct. If something seems too good to be true or the interviewer seems evasive when you ask about the company's financial stability, it may be a sign that the company is not a good fit for you.

It is always better to be cautious and do your due diligence before accepting a job offer.

HOW TO WRITE YOUR ELEVATOR PITCH?

The elevator pitch is a short promotional message presented to a targeted audience to communicate your value in 30 seconds. It's a brief way of introducing yourself, getting across a key point or two, and making a connection with someone. It's your value proposition. This also answers the famous question "Tell me about yourself?".

Job search elevator pitch: This involves marketing yourself to the hiring manager. This pitch should contain information about your career background, emphasizing why you are seeking a new opportunity and what makes you a great fit.

Networking elevator pitch: Networking is all about making connections so this version should contain a mix of professional and personal details to engage on both levels. Your pitch should help you to foster long-term relationships as well as aid your career growth.

Professional elevator pitch: A professional elevator pitch is used in situations where you describe your existing organization, product or idea to a potential client or stakeholder.

In short, the elevator pitch says who you are, what you do, who you help, what makes you unique, what main achievement or result have you had, then finishes off with a call to action; What do you want? What are you looking for? Why are you here?

Let's break it down step by step:

Step 1: Who are you? State your name, current job title, company or employment status.
Your answer:

Step 2: What do you do, what makes you unique? Identify your top three talents relevant to the role and express them. (You can add whom you help and/or a major result you've had)
Your answer:

Step 3: What are you looking for? Describe your passion and commitment to a new role, what kind of employment opportunity you are seeking, and how you can contribute.
Your answer:

The text can be changed according to the context. You should aim to write approximately 45-70 words. Start writing the oral version first. Make sure that the language you use reflects how you would speak naturally. Quite often, when we write, our language is more professional and formal than how we communicate verbally. While you want to demonstrate the best version of yourself, you want to remain true to yourself. Rehearse the pitch aloud as you write; if it doesn't sound like something that you would say, then adjust it until it flows off your tongue freely.

Once you've nailed the oral version of your elevator pitch, you can adapt this into the written statement for your job search touchpoints. Get some feedback from people you trust and polish it until you are satisfied. Practice it until it sounds natural.

Let me give you some practical examples of elevator pitches for different scenarios:

Job search elevator pitch:

Step 1: Hi, I'm Jane Doe, a Marketing Manager with 15 years of experience in leading successful campaigns for diverse clients.

Step 2: I specialize in crafting compelling content and building strong relationships with clients to ensure their satisfaction. I'm also skilled in data analysis to measure the effectiveness of campaigns.

Step 3: I'm seeking a challenging role in a dynamic company where I can utilize my skills and experience to make an impact and drive business growth.

Networking elevator pitch:

Step 1: Hi, I'm John Smith, a Sales Director at XYZ company.

Step 2: I'm passionate about connecting with people and creating meaningful relationships. My expertise lies in building effective sales strategies and coaching teams to exceed their goals. I'm also an avid traveler and food enthusiast.

Step 3: I'm always looking to expand my network and connect with like-minded professionals. Let's grab a coffee and discuss how we can help each other grow professionally.

Professional elevator pitch:

Step 1: Hi, I'm Sarah Jones, the CEO of ABC Consulting firm.

Step 2: Our firm specializes in providing innovative solutions to businesses in the healthcare industry. We've successfully helped our clients improve their operations and increase revenue. Our team is comprised of experienced professionals with diverse backgrounds.

Step 3: I'm here to explore opportunities and collaborate with other businesses and explore potential partnerships that can benefit both parties. Let's discuss how we can work together to achieve our goals.

Remember, the elevator pitch should be tailored to your audience and the context. It should highlight your strengths and communicate your value in a concise and engaging way.

HOW TO ASSESS YOUR NETWORK?

Networking may sound foreign and weird for many but it's a well-known and established practice worldwide. Some people even think that your value depends on your network.

In this exercise, you will assess your network in 4 steps:

Step1: List and rate all current contacts who CAN help you achieve your goals. These include board members, industry peers, former colleagues in executive roles or executives from other companies, industry leaders, business partners, industry experts, or influential people in your network who may have valuable connections.

Step 2: List and rate all other contacts who might NOT be able to help. Why is this important? Because, having a clear list will give a clear WHY you shouldn't be wasting your time with them. These may include former colleagues in non-executive roles, people in different industries or people you met briefly at networking events.

Step 3: Identify and rate NEW contacts who may help accomplish your goals to know who to cold contact such as executives in companies you are interested in partnering with or investors who may be interested in your company or influential people in your industry you have not yet connected with.

Step 4: Determine if any contacts listed are associated with others who can help to ask for an introduction such as business partners, board members, industry experts who may have connections with potential investors or executives at target companies or influential people in your network who may have connections with potential partners or clients.

Doing this exercise, you can use any type of rating you're comfortable with.

Here is an example:

Step 1: List and rate all current contacts who CAN help you achieve your goals.
- A former colleague who now works in a company that you're interested in. You rate this contact as a 9 out of 10.
- A mentor who has been in your industry for many years and has a lot of connections. You rate this contact as a 10 out of 10.
- A client who has expressed interest in working with you again in the future. You rate this contact as an 8 out of 10.

Step 2: List and rate all other contacts who might NOT be able to help.
- An old friend from college who is now working in a completely different field. You rate this contact as a 2 out of 10.
- A former co-worker who left the industry years ago. You rate this contact as a 3 out of 10.
- A distant relative with whom you rarely speak. You rate this contact as a 1 out of 10.

Step 3: Identify and rate NEW contacts who may help accomplish your goals to know who to cold contact.
- The CEO of a company that you're interested in. You rate this contact as a 7 out of 10.
- A recruiter who specializes in your industry. You rate this contact as a 6 out of 10.
- A keynote speaker at an upcoming conference you're attending. You rate this contact as an 8 out of 10.

Step 4: Determine if any contacts listed are associated with OTHERS who can help to ask for an introduction.
- Your mentor is connected with a prominent executive at a company you're interested in working for. You decide to reach out to your mentor for an introduction.

Equipped with knowledge, you can start researching the market with more confidence. Please do not fall into the trap of widening your search. It may be counterintuitive but won't maximize your opportunities.

Instead, you run the risk of diluting your efforts and wasting time which may demotivate you. Go for a specific city, for example, instead of a continent or a country.

WHAT IS A JOB PROPOSAL?

As a job seeker, you may find yourself in a position where you are interested in a potential job opportunity but are unsure if the role actually exists or if it aligns with your expectations and needs. In these situations, it may be possible to express your interest and clarify your expectations by submitting a candidate job proposal.

So, what is a candidate job proposal, and how can it benefit you during your job search?

A candidate job proposal is a document that outlines the specific terms and conditions that you are interested in for a potential job opportunity. It can include things like salary, benefits, vacation time, and more. By submitting a candidate job proposal, you are taking a proactive approach to the job search process and clearly communicating your expectations and needs to the employer.

But what should you include in your candidate job proposal?

Here are a few key sections to consider:

- **Introduction:** Start by introducing yourself and explaining your interest in the company.
- **Understanding of their problem**
- **Experience with previous projects:** Outline your relevant skills, experience, and qualifications for the role. (qualifications)
- **Your Vision of the solution and methods**
- **The job description of the person holding that role**

- **Expectations:** Clearly state your expectations for the role, including any specific terms and conditions you are interested in. This could include things like salary, benefits, vacation time, and more.
- **Benefits for the company**
- **Closing:** Thank the employer for considering your proposal and express your continued interest in the potential job opportunity.

Have you ever considered writing a job proposal?

Here's an example:

Title:

Executive Director, Business Development - Candidate Proposal

Introduction:

As an experienced business development professional with a proven track record of driving growth and revenue, I am excited to present my proposal for the open position of Executive Director, Business Development at ABC Corporation. I believe that my skills and experience make me uniquely qualified for this role, and I am confident that I can make a significant contribution to the success of your organization.

Understanding of their problem:

It is crucial for any business to continually identify and pursue new opportunities in order to drive growth and remain competitive in today's market. As the Executive Director, Business Development, I will be responsible for identifying and pursuing these opportunities, as well as analyzing market trends and customer data to inform strategic business development decisions. With my deep understanding of the market and the challenges facing businesses today, I am well-equipped to identify and address opportunities that will drive the success of your organization.

Experience with previous projects:

Throughout my career, I have successfully led numerous business development initiatives that have resulted in significant growth and revenue for my previous employers.

Some notable examples include:

- Identifying and securing a partnership with a major retail chain, resulting in a 50% increase in sales over a 6-month period.
- Leading the expansion of our company's presence into international markets, resulting in a 25% increase in revenue over a 3-year period.
- Developing and implementing a customer loyalty program that increased customer retention by 20% over a 1-year period.

I bring this level of experience and success to the Executive Director, Business Development role at ABC Corporation and I am confident that I can drive similar results for your organization.

Vision for the solution and methods:

As the Executive Director, Business Development, I will work to identify and pursue new business opportunities that align with the goals and values of ABC Corporation. This may include partnerships, acquisitions, or market expansion. My approach to business development will be data-driven, with a strong focus on analyzing market trends and customer data to inform strategic decisions. I will also work closely with other departments, including sales, marketing, and product development, to ensure that new business ventures are successfully implemented.

In order to cultivate relationships with potential partners and clients, I will utilize my strong communication and negotiation skills, as well as my ability to build trust and establish long-term partnerships. I will also lead and manage a team of business development professionals, ensuring that we are working collaboratively and efficiently to achieve our goals.

Job Description:

Responsibilities:

- Develop and implement long-term business development strategies to drive growth and revenue.
- Identify and pursue new business opportunities, including partnerships, acquisitions, and market expansion.
- Cultivate relationships with potential partners and clients, and negotiate contracts to close deals.
- Collaborate with other departments, including sales, marketing, and product development, to ensure successful implementation of new business ventures.
- Analyze market trends and customer data to inform business development decisions.
- Lead and manage a team of business development professionals.

Required qualifications:

- Master's degree in Business or related field.
- 7 to10 years of experience in business development, with at least 5 years in a leadership role.
- Strong communication and negotiation skills.
- Proven track record of successful business development.
- Ability to analyze market trends and customer data.
- Excellent leadership and management abilities.

Benefits for the company:

As the Executive Director, Business Development, I will be responsible for driving the growth and success of your organization through the identification and pursuit of new business opportunities. My experience in cultivating relationships with potential partners and clients, negotiating contracts, and leading a team of business development professionals will enable me to significantly expand your reach and increase revenue. Additionally, my expertise and experience in the field will help your organization to effectively implement new business ventures and stay ahead of market trends.

Compensation and benefits package:

Salary: $150,000 per year.

Additional perks:
- Health insurance.
- Retirement benefits.
- 4 weeks of vacation time per year.
- Performance-based bonuses.
- Professional development opportunities.

Closing statement:

I am confident that my skills and experience make me the ideal candidate for the Executive Director, Business Development position at ABC Corporation. I am excited about the opportunity to contribute to the success of your organization and I am eager to discuss this proposal further.

Thank you for considering my application.
Sincerely, [Your name]

HOW TO RECOGNIZE
DISCRIMINATORY PRACTICES?

Discrimination in the workplace is illegal and can take many forms, including discrimination based on race, gender, age, religion, and more. As a job seeker, it's important to be aware of these types of discriminatory practices and to know what to do if you encounter them.

So how can you recognize discriminatory practices during your job search? Here are a few things to look out for:

Job postings that include discriminatory language: If a job posting includes language that seems to exclude certain groups of people, this may be a red flag. For example, a job posting that requires applicants to have a degree from a "top school" can be seen as elitism bias.

Interview questions that seem inappropriate: During an interview, you should be asked about your qualifications and experience, not about your personal life or characteristics such as your age, religion, or family status. If you are asked inappropriate questions, this may be a sign of discrimination or pure ignorance. Questions about family status such as "Do you have children?" or "Do you plan on having more children?" are inappropriate and can be seen as discriminatory. Questions about age, race, national origin, gender, religion, marital status and sexual orientation are off-limits by law in many countries.

Different treatment during the hiring process: If you feel like you are being treated differently than other candidates during the hiring process, this may be a sign of discrimination. For example, if you are not given the same opportunities or consideration as other candidates, this could be a problem or requiring all minority applicants to take an employment test while not requiring the same of non-minority applicants.

If you encounter any of these red flags during your job search, it's important to know what to do. Here are a few steps you can take:

Document the situation: Keep a record of any discriminatory experiences you have, including details about what happened and who was involved. This can be helpful if you need to report the issue or take legal action.

Seek support: Don't suffer in silence. Reach out to a trusted friend, family member, or professional counselor for support. It can also be helpful to join a support group or network with others who have experienced similar situations.

Report the issue: If you feel comfortable doing so, consider reporting the issue to HR or management. You may also want to consider reaching out to an employment lawyer or a civil rights organization for assistance.

Consider your other options: If the issue cannot be resolved, you may need to consider applying elsewhere. You don't want to join a company that doesn't want you anyway. It's important to prioritize your own well-being and to work in a positive and inclusive environment.

By being aware of discriminatory practices and knowing what to do if you encounter them, you can help to create a more equal and just workplace for yourself and for others.

My Thoughts On Ageism

Many senior clients reach out to me asking whether they are too late in their life to look for a job or to switch careers or to become an entrepreneur.

The short answer is: No.

Being laid off at 40, 50 or 60+ is never easy. Although you may notice discriminatory practices related to ageism, there are always ways to address the issue.

The question here would be: What are you doing to remain relevant? Here are a few ideas to get you started:

- **Your education is at least 15 years old:** Educate yourself on what the companies are looking for in terms of non-negotiable education and certification. You might bridge the gap with online micro-lessons or go back to school and get a more recent diploma or certification.

- **Your tech skills are not up-to-date:** Technology is evolving very fast and companies are pressed to adopt the newest ones or risk going out of business. See what your gaps are and take action. You don't want to be left behind in the digital age. Enroll in online courses, attend workshops or seminars, and familiarize yourself with relevant software or tools used in your desired field. Demonstrating proficiency in modern technology will enhance your marketability and show potential employers that you can adapt to their evolving needs.

- **You are only working with seniors:** Consider mentoring younger individuals in your field. Share your knowledge, experiences, and insights with the next generation. Becoming a mentor not only allows you to contribute to the development of others but also keeps you engaged with current trends and perspectives. It demonstrates your commitment to continuous learning and collaboration.

In short, speak about how you are the solution to the employer's problem today. If you introduced innovation in your old company or helped the team to adapt to a major change, definitely speak to those!

SECTION FOUR
BOUNCING BACK FASTER AND STRONGER:
HARNESSING MOTIVATION FOR SUCCESS

HOW TO DEAL AND COPE WITH GRIEF?

Losing a job or changing jobs and relocating can be a source of grief and loss, and the job search process itself can be a difficult and emotionally draining experience. It's important to recognize and cope with these emotions in order to move forward in your job search and your career. Grief is a natural response to loss. Let's explore the stages of grief that may arise during your job search and provide you with some coping strategies.

Denial: In the denial stage, you may find it difficult to accept the loss of your job and may struggle to take action in your job search. You may feel overwhelmed or numb and may try to push aside your emotions in order to cope.

Anger: The anger stage is characterized by feelings of frustration, anger, and resentment. You may feel angry at yourself, your employer, or the situation that led to your job loss. This can make it difficult to focus on your job search and make decisions.

Bargaining: In the bargaining stage, you may find yourself trying to negotiate or make deals in order to avoid the reality of your situation. You may find yourself thinking things like, "If I had just worked harder, maybe I wouldn't have lost my job," or "If I can just find a similar job quickly, everything will be okay."

Depression: The depression stage is characterized by feelings of sadness, hopelessness, and a lack of motivation. You may find it difficult to get out of bed in the morning or to engage in activities that you normally enjoy.

Acceptance: In the acceptance stage, you are able to acknowledge and accept the reality of your situation. You may still experience grief and sadness, but you are able to move forward and take steps to rebuild your career.

Everyone experiences grief differently, and you may move through these stages in a different order or at a different pace. Please recognize that it's okay to feel a wide range of emotions during this process and that it's normal to feel like you are moving backwards at times.

It's natural to feel demotivated and discouraged during the job search process, especially when dealing with grief and loss. However, it's crucial to stay motivated and persistent in order to find a job that is a good fit for your skills and career goals.

Here are a few strategies for staying motivated and persistent when you are dealing with grief:

Set goals: Setting goals can help to keep you focused and motivated. Make sure to set both short-term goals and long-term goals, and celebrate small victories along the way.

Seek out resources and support: There are many resources and support systems available to help you during the job search process. This may include hiring a coach or strategist, joining professional organizations or online groups for job seekers, or participating in job fairs and networking events.

Find ways to reframe your perspective: Reframing can help you stay positive. This may involve reminding yourself of your strengths and accomplishments or finding ways to see your job loss as an opportunity for growth and change.

Participate in activities that bring you joy and purpose: Continue to engage in activities that bring you joy and purpose, even when you are feeling down. This can help to boost your mood and give you a sense of accomplishment.

Take care of yourself: Prioritize self-care during this time. Make sure to get enough sleep, eat well, and engage in physical activity. It can also be helpful to set boundaries and make time for activities that help you relax and de-stress

It's okay to take your time. Give yourself time to grieve and process your feelings. Don't be afraid to take breaks or adjust your job search pace as needed.

HOW TO STAY MOTIVATED DURING A JOB SEARCH?

Finding a job can be a challenging and often frustrating process. Remember that job search is a marathon, not a sprint, and it's vital to stay motivated and persistent in order to achieve your career goals. Here are some tips:

Set clear goals: Have a clear idea of what you want to achieve with your job search. Setting specific and measurable goals can help to keep you focused and motivated. For example, instead of just setting a goal to "find a job," try setting a goal to apply to at least 10 jobs per week or to network with at least 3 new people each week.

Create a schedule: Establishing a consistent job search routine can help to keep you on track and motivated. Set aside a specific time each day or week to focus on your job search, and be sure to include time for networking, applying to jobs, and updating your resume and cover letter.

Seek out support: Surround yourself with supportive people who can help to keep you motivated and offer encouragement when you're feeling down. This can include friends, family, colleagues, or even a career coach.

Take breaks: It's easy to become burnt out when you're constantly focused on your job search. Be sure to take breaks and give yourself time to relax and recharge. This can help to prevent burnout and keep you motivated in the long run.

Focus on your accomplishments: Remember that job search is a process, and it's normal to experience setbacks along the way. Instead of dwelling on rejections, try to focus on the things that you have accomplished so far, such as networking with new people or learning new skills.

Celebrate small victories: Celebrate your successes, no matter how small they may seem. This can help to keep you motivated and give you a sense of accomplishment.

Keep perspective: It's easy to become discouraged when you're not receiving job offers. Keep perspective and remind yourself that it's normal to go through a period of rejection before finding the right job.

Stay positive: Maintain a positive attitude and stay hopeful, even when things are not going as planned. This can help to keep you motivated and prevent you from becoming discouraged.

Learn from your experiences: Every job search experience is an opportunity to learn and grow. Take away valuable lessons from each interview or networking event, and use that knowledge to improve your job search strategy.

By following these tips, you can stay motivated and persistent during your job search, and eventually land the job of your dreams. Remember to keep an open mind, and don't be afraid to ask for help when you need it.

HOW TO EVALUATE YOUR JOB SEARCH STRATEGY?

Let's Start With A Distinction

Throughout the years, I have observed a misconception between perseverance and knowing when stop doing something in the context of a job search. Let me explain:

Perseverance is the quality of persisting in your efforts despite challenges, setbacks, or rejections. In the job search context, it means staying resilient and determined in pursuing opportunities, even when faced with obstacles. Perseverance is vital because job searches can be lengthy, competitive, and occasionally disheartening. It requires maintaining a positive mindset, learning from failures, and continually adapting your strategies to improve your chances of success.

Knowing when to stop doing something in a job search refers to recognizing when a particular strategy, approach, or target is no longer effective or aligned with your goals. It involves assessing the return on investment (ROI) of your efforts and making informed decisions to discontinue or redirect your actions. It requires being self-aware, flexible, and willing to pivot when necessary.

While perseverance is essential, blindly persisting in an ineffective or unproductive approach can lead to wasted time, energy, and opportunities.

So, regularly assess and evaluate the outcomes of your job search activities, be open to feedback and external input, and be willing to adjust your strategies accordingly.

Here are some indicators to consider:

- **Lack of results:** If you've been consistently applying for jobs or pursuing certain strategies without receiving positive responses or progressing in the hiring process, it may be a sign to reassess your career documents, your message, your methods, and try alternative approaches.

- **Market feedback:** Pay attention to the feedback you receive from employers, recruiters, or industry professionals. If there's consistent feedback indicating gaps in your qualifications or a mismatch between your goals and the job market, it may be time for a re-evaluation.

- **Personal well-being:** If the job search process becomes excessively stressful, negatively impacting your self-esteem or overall happiness, stop and consider whether your current strategies are sustainable and if adjustments are needed.

- **Lack of alignment:** If your job search activities are not aligned with your career goals, values, or long-term aspirations, it may be time to reassess and redirect your efforts toward opportunities that better align with your desired path.

- **External factors:** Changes in the job market, industry trends, or personal circumstances can also influence when it's appropriate to adjust your job search approach. Staying aware of these factors and being responsive to them can help you make timely decisions.

Track Your Networking Activities

I highly recommend tracking all the interactions you have because after a while it's going to be hard to remember what was said to whom and when to follow up.

You're also going to speak with a big number of people which will be hard to manage.

Create a tracking system using any tool you're comfortable with including the information: Name, Position, Company, Source/Referred by, Date of contact, Topic, To follow-up Yes/No, If Yes to follow-up on (date)

Track Your Job Applications

Another thing I also observed, is that job seekers tend to press the apply button on different platforms without a centralized tracking system to see what's going on and avoid applying more than once to the same job at the same company.

Create a tracking system using any tool you're comfortable with again but this time including information related to the progress of your job applications: Company, Position, Salary, Source/Referred by, Application date, Contact (Name, Email, Phone number), Response, Interview details, Offer

Make sure you also keep the following information for each application:
- The text of the job post you applied to online (because they disappear later) in a folder (You can copy/paste it into a Word document)
- The version on the Resume/CV you used
- The name and contact details of the referral if any

Track Your Weekly Activity

Track your activity for a week noting how much time you're allocating for your activity for each day of the week and mentioning whether it was job search-related or not.

This will give you an overview of what you're doing and you'll be able to judge whether it is too little to yield consistency and results or too much and overwhelming.

Evaluate Your Job Search Strategy

Evaluation is usually defined as the making of a judgement about the amount, number, or value of something which is also known as assessment. It's a method that helps increase the chances of reaching your goals and know where you will need to allocate your energy.

Evaluating your job search at different stages is often overlooked and this can cause a dilution of your efforts when your objective is to shorten the time spent.

It will help you gather critical information that will support further decision making and help you focus your energy on the most fruitful activities.

Doing this exercise will help you become thorough, methodic, and consistent in your job search.

The questions will also guide you to know what kind of activities you should be doing. I highly recommend using the job search evaluation checklist to make sure you have all the tools you need and take steps towards success.

Remember that you can always hire a professional as your accountability partner to guide you as job search can be overwhelming.

By the end of this activity, you will know exactly what you need to do to perfect your job search and get the results you are looking for.

This is also an opportunity to remind you to take a wholistic methodology.

Some of the items are directly related to parts that are not covered here, but I want to give you the whole picture despite that.

Answer with a Yes or No:

- I have completed my career exploration and I am clear about myself and my target. *Your Answer:*

- I am clear about the role, salary, industry, and country I am interested in. *Your Answer:*

- I am aware of any required equivalency or board/association membership as well as work authorization. *Your Answer:*

- I know how to look for labour market information and I researched the employment laws applicable to my case. *Your Answer:*

- I am clear about my career brand and people can recognize it. *Your Answer:*

- I have an articulated elevator pitch and a value proposition that I can communicate both in writing and verbally. *Your Answer:*

- My Résumé, Cover Letter, and LinkedIn profile conform to the modern standards in terms of content and design. *Your Answer:*

- I have employment letters from every job I mention on my Résumé, Cover Letter, and LinkedIn. *Your Answer:*

- I have proof of any education and certification I mention on my Résumé, Cover Letter, and LinkedIn profile. *Your Answer:*

- I have secured between three to five references that can speak to my advantage and I keep contact with them. *Your Answer:*

- I have thoroughly prepared for interviews, went through all types of questions, got feedback, and have a number of stories ready. *Your Answer:*

- I looked my name up online, checked, and dealt with any unsatisfactory search result. *Your Answer:*

- I send a personalized cover letter wherever it is required and I don't when it is explicitly not required. *Your Answer:*

- I am generating relevant content to showcase my expertise and I am engaging with other professionals in the industry I am interested in. *Your Answer:*

- I identified at least ten companies to target in my job search and researched them well. *Your Answer:*

- I am connecting and engaging with a number of people in each company I identified by asking for informational interviews. *Your Answer:*

- I know how to prepare for informational interviews and I know what to do before, during, and after them. *Your Answer:*

- I am expanding my professional network, attending industry-related events to learn more about people and opportunities. *Your Answer:*

- I am avoiding solely relying on job boards and company career websites to apply for jobs. *Your Answer:*

- I have a networking contact, job application, and interviews tracking systems in place and I keep them updated. *Your Answer:*

- I can recognize any discriminatory activity taking place during my job search or during interviews. *Your Answer:*

- I send thank you notes to each person I meet whether for networking or for an interview after 24 hours. *Your Answer:*

- I am taking care of my mental and physical health and engaging in activities that help me regulate my stress. *Your Answer:*

- I can assess if a job offer is suitable and fits my needs. I know how to negotiate both the salary and the benefits. *Your Answer:*

You are now able to identify what's missing and adjust accordingly.

BONUS

HOW TO OVERCOME WORK AUTHORIZATION BARRIERS?

If you are looking for a job where you do not have a work authorization to worry about, great; you can skip this chapter. But if you are looking for a job abroad then be aware that each country has its own rules and regulations. Depending on your circumstances, you will need to see what applies to you.

This step is very important because it will give you an indication of which countries to consider and what benefits could look like enabling you to negotiate to your advantage.

Please, please, please! Make sure you read the employment laws of the country you're interested to relocate to. It will help avoid any bad surprises.

Here are seven ways to look at this topic and complement your job search strategy:

You work in a multinational and there's a vacancy elsewhere: Check the internal rotation rules. Please note that some multinationals can do this, while others cannot for legal reasons.

What you do is in high demand: Companies can't find employees locally or regionally and they're ready to pay for a work visa. Please note that this requires networking skills.

There are work-friendly countries around you: Look for a job in neighbouring countries with which your country has strong "positive" ties and accessible work visa conditions. Please note that these may change with politics.

You are interested to work with a global company: Apply to international companies or NGOs already known for hiring international candidates. Please note that the process can be very competitive.

You prefer to take tiny steps: Start with remote work/contract/project-based jobs/projects with companies that do not have location limitations because there's always a chance for things to change when the company experiences your work. Please note that this helps get your skills known to more people inside the company, which is very positive.

You need to see a list first: Knowing that employers need a permit before they can sponsor a foreign worker, many countries post a list with their names. Please note that the number of countries that do that is very limited.

You prefer to immigrate: Apply for an immigration program (if available) that allows you to work in the country you're targeting.

WHAT ARE FACTORS TO CONSIDER IN AN INTERNATIONAL JOB RELOCATION?

When looking for an international job relocation, there are several factors you may want to consider.

Is your job regulated? Many industries and professions have specific regulations and requirements that must be met to work in that field, and failure to comply with these regulations can result in terrible consequences. Be aware that meeting the local requirements may take a few months or a few years, which may mean that you have to go back to school and/or pass exams. For example, Canada is one of the most regulated countries in the world and most professions need certain certifications. Check this website for more information: The Canadian Information Centre for International Credentials https://www.cicic.ca/928/find_out_if_your_occupation_is_regulated_or_not.canada

What is the cost of living like? The cost of living can vary greatly from country to country. Research the cost of housing, food, and other necessities in your new location to ensure that you can afford to live there. Some salaries may not be enough to cover rent! And please make sure you relocate with enough money to get by until you find a job or get paid. Expenses can be really high when you rent an unfurnished home, for example. To see numbers, you can check
- Numbeo: https://www.numbeo.com/cost-of-living/
- WorldData: https://www.worlddata.info/cost-of-living.php
- Expatisan: https://www.expatistan.com/cost-of-living/country

What is the political climate like? Be aware of any ongoing political conflicts or tensions, as well as any human rights concern, that may affect your safety, access to services, and well-being.

What are the job market and economic conditions like? Research the job market and determine whether there are opportunities for advancement and professional development in your field. Understand the economy including the overall stability and growth, as well as the exchange rate and inflation rate, which can affect your purchasing power and the cost of living. Millions in local currency may translate into a few hundred American dollars. For example, when it comes to Labour Market Information in Canada, you have access to a number of resources such as:
- Labour Market Information Council: https://lmic-cimt.ca/
- Job Bank: https://www.jobbank.gc.ca/trend-analysis
- Labour Statistics: https://www.statcan.gc.ca/en/subjects-start/labour_

What is the availability of healthcare, medical, and emergency services like? The quality of healthcare can vary from one country to another. Research the availability and cost of medical care in your new location, particularly if you have any pre-existing medical conditions. In some countries, you may have very limited choices.

What are the cultural and social norms like? Every country has its cultural customs and ways of doing things. Be prepared for the differences. Research the country's customs, social norms and etiquette to avoid misunderstandings or cultural faux pas. It might also be a good idea to locate the community or associations of the nationality you belong to, to help with orientation. You can visit websites like:
- EveryCulture: https://www.everyculture.com/
- Hofstede Insights: https://www.hofstede-insights.com/

What are the cultural differences like? In terms of work-life balance and what is considered professional, some countries may have a more relaxed attitude towards working hours and vacation time, while others may have a more formal and structured approach to work. Research these cultural differences to prepare for them and to set expectations accordingly.

What is the language spoken? Knowing the language will be of great help in terms of communication and integration. Even if the job position doesn't require a high proficiency in the language, communicating with colleagues or customers will be essential for your day-to-day work and personal life. Many companies provide language classes to help employees improve their language skills, but it would be good to have a basic knowledge before relocating. You can get started with a mobile app like Duolingo: https://www.duolingo.com/

What is the available support for families like? If you are moving with your family, research the availability of schools, childcare services, and support for families in your new location. You may want to ask about language support and the possibility to exempt your child from certain classes. In some countries, international schools are available, however, the cost may be prohibitive.

How your international job relocation might affect your current social and professional networks? You will be leaving behind friends, family, and professional connections that are familiar and valuable. It may take time to build a new network in your new location. Stay connected with these people should you decide to go back and seek out new connections in your new location.

What is the company you're looking to work with like? Gather as much information about its history, culture, financial stability, reputation, and working conditions. Knowing the background can help you to decide if it's a good fit for you, and it can also give you an idea of what to expect when it comes to the company's management, values, and overall working environment but also if the job is a scam. Some websites like Glassdoor: https://www.glassdoor.com/ offer employee reviews.

What are the working conditions like? Investigate the working conditions, including the hours, benefits, and pay of the job. Different countries have different regulations and standards for working hours and minimum wage. It will help assess if a work contract is good enough for you. In some countries, you may not have access to rent for a certain amount per month if you are not making a certain amount per year and in some other countries, you may be sponsored with your family while in others, you may not. For Canada, you can research "Canadian Employment Standards" on a Federal and Provincial level or the European Union: https://ec.europa.eu/social/main.jsp?catId=157&langId=en for labour law in the EU.

What is the availability of professional development and training opportunities like? This can be a determining factor to keep your skills updated and enhance your future career prospects. Some companies may provide training and development opportunities to help you adjust to your new location and improve your skills.

What are the tax laws and regulations like? Every country has its own tax laws. Research and understand how these laws will affect your income and expenses. Consider whether there are any tax treaties as these can affect your tax liability. Expatica: https://www.expatica.com/ has a wealth of information about this and other topics.

What are the laws and regulations related to work permits and visas? The process of obtaining a work permit or visa can be time-consuming and complicated, and you will need to understand the requirements and be aware of any potential delays. Seek professional advice on the move; you might see your passport withheld by the employer in certain countries. Note that changing employers later may not be as easy as you think; the workflow may require permissions and clearances while other countries have a list of companies that can sponsor visas such as:
- UK: https://www.gov.uk/government/publications/register-of-licensed-sponsors-workers
- Netherlands: https://ind.nl/en/public-register-recognised-sponsors?fbclid=IwAR3Q2RJtulOucl8tv0uo2M9YPcWIUxiXyk8f6y0iG WnlYbnc-0iTPkUw61w

What are the social security and pension system like? Research the social security system and determine whether you will be eligible for benefits and how they compare to your current country. Depending on the country you might have to make contributions without having access to any benefits and might need to have a different approach to your retirement plan.

What is the availability and cost of transportation like? If you need to commute to work daily, you will want to see the availability and cost of public vs private transportation. For example, can you drive in that country with your current driving license? If you are taking the bus, make sure to check the days and schedules of the buses close to your location. Also look into the availability of other services such as banking, grocery stores and other daily necessities. This will be crucial for your daily life and for you to be able to maintain a certain level of comfort and familiarity.

What will be the impact of international job relocation on your personal life? The move will likely involve significant changes and adjustments for you and your family. You might have decided to leave your family in your home country or might have decided to relocate as a family; whatever the scenario is, be prepared for these changes and to have a plan in place to support yourself and your loved ones through the transition.

What is the availability and quality of housing like? Research the different neighbourhoods and areas, and the cost of renting or buying a property. Some countries may have stricter regulations for rental properties and more competition for affordable housing while others don't allow expats to buy property.

What is the internet and phone service like? Research the quality, availability and cost of internet and phone services as they can be vital to staying connected with family and friends, as well as for work and personal use.

What is the availability of recreational activities and leisure time options like? Finding ways to relax and enjoy your free time is an important aspect of the moving experience. Having access to recreational activities and entertainment options can help make the transition to your new location smoother. With some jobs, you might find yourself in the middle of nowhere like the sea or the desert living in a structure or a compound.

What is the accessibility of services for people with disabilities or special needs like? Research the availability of accommodations and support services like transportation, education, healthcare, and housing options. In some countries, being in a wheelchair is a curse while in others the infrastructure is there to help live as independently as possible.

What is the availability of pet-friendly housing options, or the regulations and the cost of bringing your pet with you like? If you have a pet and you're planning to bring it with you, investigate the laws, and regulations that might be required before you bring your pet as some countries have banned certain types and certain breeds.

What is the availability of insurance options like? Check the availability of health, life, and property insurance, as well as other types of insurance that may be necessary for your specific situation. In some countries, the cost is so high that it requires a budget.

What is the availability of legal services and resources like? Things like finding a lawyer, accessing legal information, and understanding the legal system. In some countries, expats are treated differently than locals.

What will the future of living in that country look like? Some countries offer nationality after a certain number of years while others do not. Whether you are leaving to work for a few years and later coming back, or to stay permanently in the county, take into account the future that is fit for you and your family.

Researching these factors will help you make a well-informed decision about your international job relocation and ensure that you are prepared for the changes that come with it.

CONCLUSION

That's it for the job search part!

Now, you have a solid plan with a number of action steps. Depending on the variables at play, you may land a job in a day (Yes, it's possible, I've seen it with some of my clients) or you may need one or more months.

Remember that you are responsible for your own job search. You are the Project Manager of your job search. No one can do it on your behalf. Recruitment and placement agencies only work with companies who have vacancies and they are accountable to whoever employs them. That's why it's paramount to have a plan.

Job search is a marathon, it's complex and needs to be managed step by step, day by day, week after week to make it quicker, faster, and shorter. That's how you create momentum and consistency.

You may be currently employed while looking for your next career move. You may have lost your job and found yourself forced to look for something else. Maybe you didn't work for a while and you decided to come back. Or maybe you have a company but the economy is dire and you need to supplement your income.

Whatever your case is, you will hear a lot of "No", you might engage in certain actions and hear nothing back (and even more so when there is a visa authorization barrier to overcome). Please don't let that deter you, persevere. Even when you land the job, keep going, stay informed, and be up to date with the job market.

Job search in itself is a job. Some days may feel like a slap on the face and may be tough mentally, please take all the time you need, and take care of yourself.

I know what it feels like to look for a job, to face adversity, and uncertainty, I've been there. Every month without a job is a month of salary lost; if you are in a critical financial situation, it's hard and bitter. I've been there too.

That's why I believe that job search is a life skill. Think about it: it can bring you a better offer, a better title, a relocation, or a new lifestyle. It can literally change your life. How valuable and precious is that?

Job search is a process and I encourage you to be intentional about it. It starts by knowing what you want, creating career documents of a high standard, executing the job search plan, and finally, interviewing. You see, you need to communicate a consistent message throughout. It's part of your personal branding and marketing.

More than 15 years of experience later, I find myself learning every single day. I've been in the market and I've seen that market change over and over again. I've had the opportunity to work with brilliant professionals from different countries. Some were searching for a job locally while others were looking to relocate. Some wanted to change something about their job, whereas others were seeking to move up the ladder.
When it comes to testimonials, I have plenty on my website: http://dossierpro.co/ This book is the framework I use during the private one-on-one live sessions.

The difference is the live feedback, the accessibility to technical and emotional support, accountability, and follow-up. If you'd like to add these pieces, send me a message: https://www.dossierpro.co/contact/ or an email: rita@dossierpro.co.

I'm curious, what was your biggest takeaway from this book?

Have you had any breakthroughs?

Did you take action and implement the steps?

Please share feedback and your progress with me, I'd love to hear about it!

Be well and bye for now.

May I ask you something?

If you liked the book and would like to support me to make it available to as many people who need it as possible during these difficult times, I would be very grateful if you would take a few seconds to write a review.

Thank you very much for reading!

ABOUT THE AUTHOR

Rita Kamel

Career Development Practitioner (CDP) | Master Certified Career Strategist (MCCS) | Master Certified Employment Strategist (MCES) | Award-Winning Certified Resume Strategist (CRS) and Certified Interview Strategist (CIS) | Certified Work-Life Strategist (CWS) | Founder of DossierPro: http://www.dossierpro.co/

I believe powerful questions can inspire immediate action. I will help you identify and promote your unique value proposition and personal branding to empower you to lead your international career moves.

I am a multi-awarded and multi-certified Career Development Practitioner fluent in English, French, and Arabic. I have coached established senior professionals since 2006 and have extensive recruitment experience in the MENA region, Europe, and Canada, which I use to help clients navigate international job searches and overcome barriers.

I have seen talented people go unrecognized and unappreciated for too long, and I am committed to helping them succeed. My services range from providing a 360° view of the employment space by sharing the ins and outs of the recruitment process, guiding clients to figure out their careers, writing targeted documents, empowering them during job search, and preparing for their interviews.

I am eager to help you create career opportunities around the world! Connect me on social media:
- Rita Kamel @ritakml
- DossierPro: @dossierproco

NOTES